Music from Disney

FROZEN

arranged for harp by Sylvia Woods

CONTENTS:

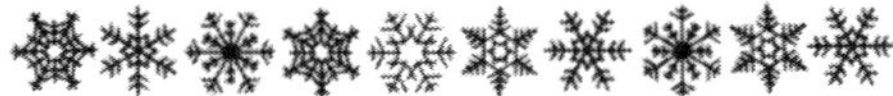

Here are the harp string ranges needed for the 3 pieces.

Let It Go

Range of 29 strings from very low E to very high E.
C, F, and G accidentals.

Do You Want to Build a Snowman?

Basic range of 28 strings from very low A to very high D. There are two notes that go up to the higher G and A (shown here in parentheses), but these are octave notes that may be omitted if necessary.
C, G, and A accidentals.

IMPORTANT NOTE IF YOU TUNE YOUR LEVER HARP TO 3 FLATS:
You will need to retune the A above middle C and the very low A (9 strings below middle C) to naturals with your tuning key, so that you will be able to make A sharps in this arrangement.

Heimr Árnadalr

Range of 20 strings from very low G to high E.
F accidentals.

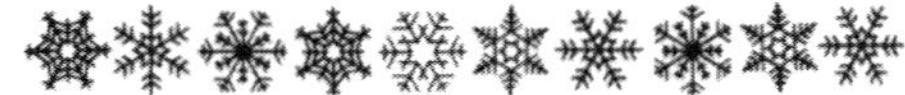

Let It Go

From Disney FROZEN

Music and Lyrics by KRISTEN ANDERSON-LOPEZ
and ROBERT LOPEZ

Harp Arrangement by SYLVIA WOODS

Lever harp players: Set your sharping levers for the key signature, and then re-set the levers shown above.
Sharping lever changes are indicated with diamond notes and also with octave wording.
Pedal changes are written below the bass staff.

Half-time feel, mysterious

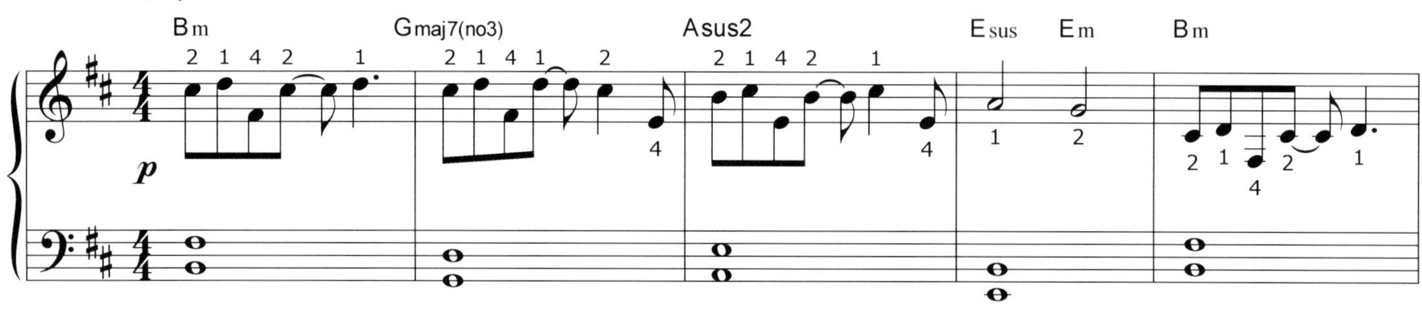

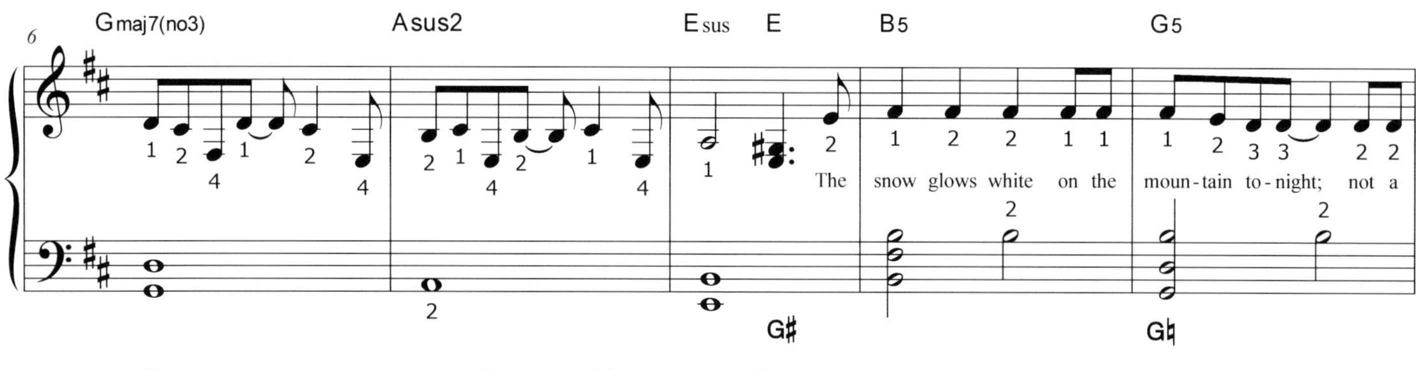

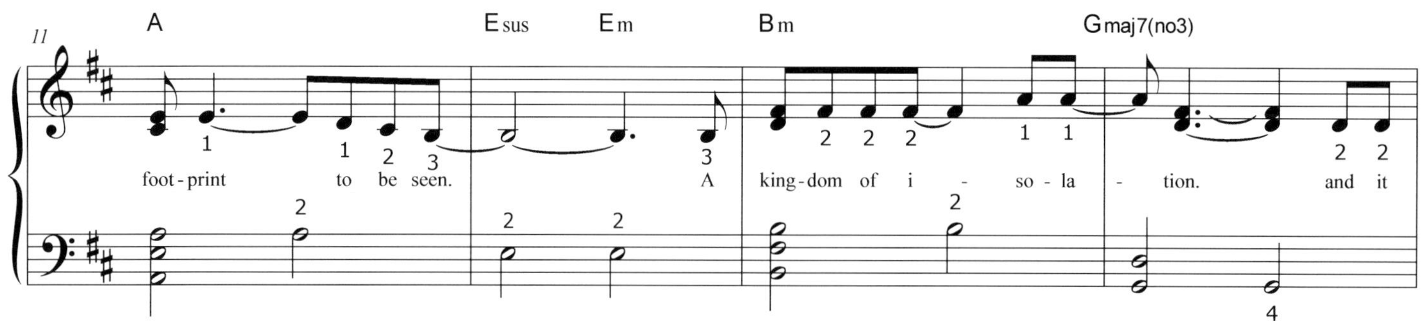

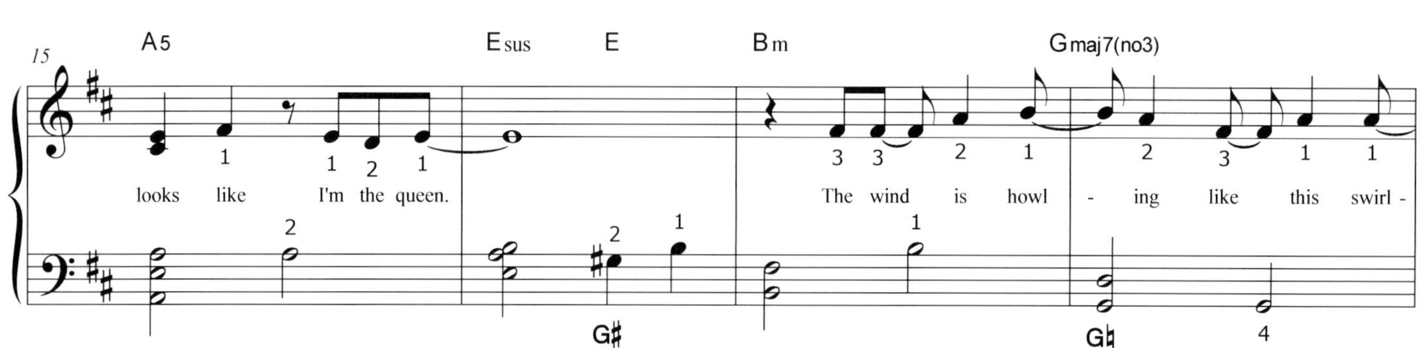

19
Asus2 Esus Em B5 A5
- ing storm in - side. Could - n't keep it in, heav - en knows I
23
E Esus2 E A
tried. Don't let them in, don't let them see;
G♯ G♮
27
G A
be the good girl you al - ways have to be. Con - ceal, don't feel, don't let them know.
31
G
Well, now they know. Let it go,
35
D A Bm G
let it go, can't hold it back an - y - more. Let it go,

39
D A Bm G
let it go; turn a-way and slam the door.
43
D A Bm G
I don't care what they're going to say; let the
middle C♮
47
F♯m F G5
storm rage on. The cold nev-er both-ered me an-y-way.
middle C♯
F♮
C♮
F♯
51
D A/C♯ Bm G
It's fun-ny how some dis-tance makes
C♯
55
A Em Bm A
ev-'ry-thing seem small; and the fears that once con-trolled me can't

59
Em
E
A
get to me at all.
It's time to see what I can do,
G♯
G♮
63
G
A
to test the lim - its and break through.
No right, no wrong, no rules for me,
67
G
D
I'm free!
Let it go, let it go,
71
A
Bm
G
D
I am one with the wind and sky.
Let it go, let it go,
75
A
Bm
G
D
A
you'll nev - er see me cry.
Here I stand,

Bm G F♯m F
middle C♮
and here I'll stay; let the storm rage on.
F♮ C♮
N.C.
high C♮ high F♮
play with right hand as necessary for lever changes
My pow - er flur - ries through the air in - to the ground.
F♯ F♮
My soul is spi - ral - ing in fro - zen frac - tals all a - round.
mid G♯ high C♯
F♯ F♮
And one thought cry - stal - li - zes like an i - cy blast:
high F♯
B Gmaj7
mf I'm nev - er go -
G♯ F♯ C♯ G♮

A Em G D
- - ing back, the past is in the past!
mid G♮
ff
Let it go, let it go,
A Bm G D
and I'll rise like the break of dawn. Let it go, let it go,
A Bm G D A
that per - fect girl is gone. Here I stand
Bm G F♯m F
low C♮
in the light of day; let the storm rage on.
F♮
C♮
Gsus2
mp
The cold nev - er both - ered me an - y - way.
F♯

Do You Want to Build a Snowman?

From Disney FROZEN

Music and Lyrics by KRISTEN ANDERSON-LOPEZ
and ROBERT LOPEZ

Harp Arrangement by SYLVIA WOODS

Lever harp players: Set your sharping levers for the key signature, and then re-set the levers shown above.

Important note if you tune your lever harp to 3 flats: You will need to retune the A above middle C and the very low A (9 strings below middle C) to A naturals with your tuning key, so that you will be able to make A sharps in this arrangement.

Moderate; rhythmic but expressive

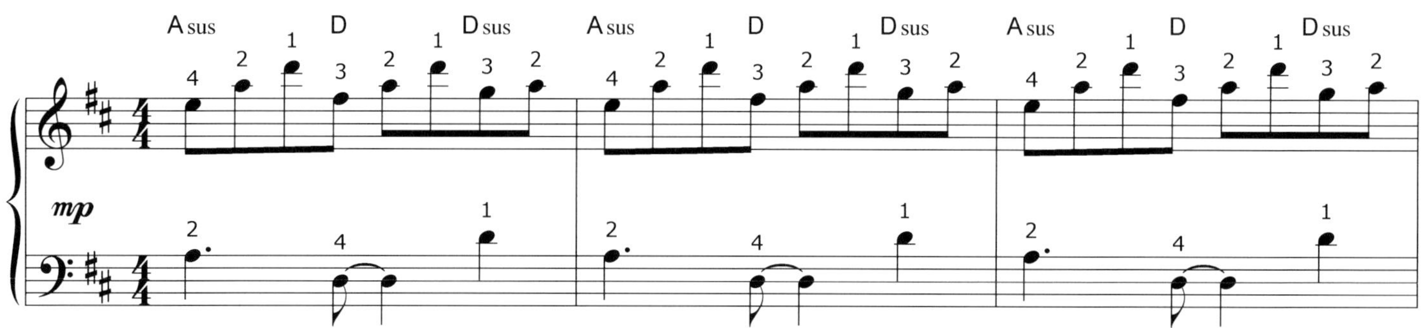

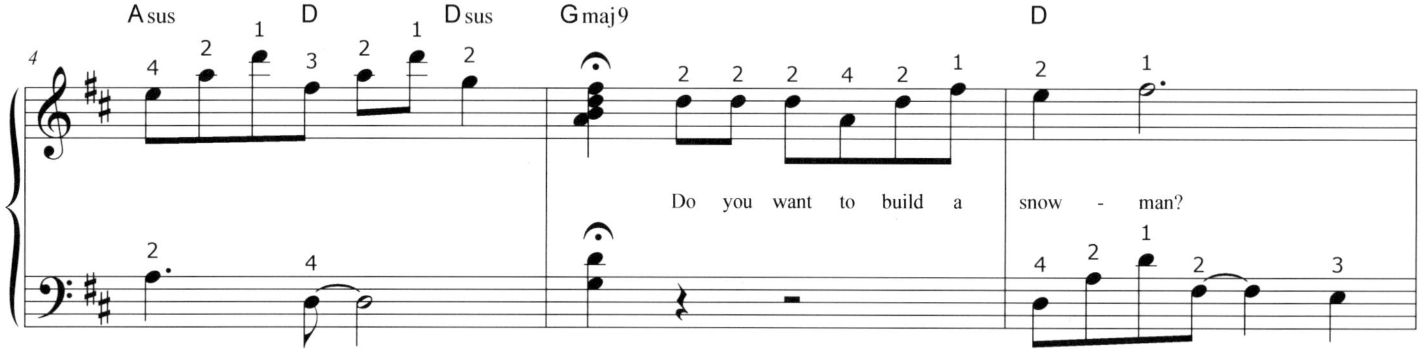

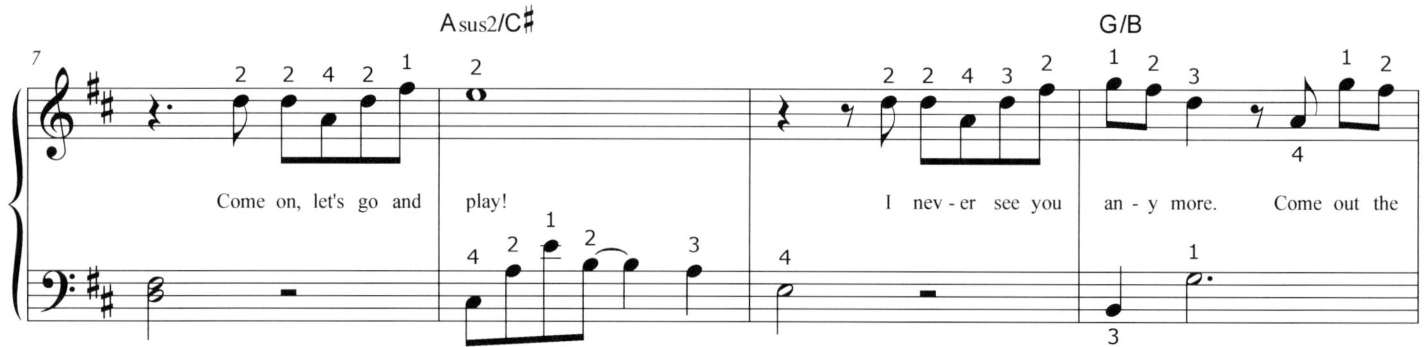

Bm
Am(add2)
D/F♯
door! It's like you've gone a - way.
We used to be best
C♮
G(add2)
F♯m7
Gmaj7/C♯
F♯7
bud - dies, and now were not. I wish you would tell me
C♯
Bm
E7
Em9
why. Do you want to build a snow - man? It does-n't have to be a
G♯
G♮
Gm6/B♭
snow - man.
ELSA: (Spoken)
Go away Anna
O - kay, bye.
D
A♯
A♮
Gmaj9
mf
Do you want to build a

D
Asus2/C♯
snow - man? Or ride our bike a-round the halls? I think some com-pan - y is
G/B
Bm
Am
o - ver - due; I've start - ed talk - ing to the pic - tures on the walls.
C♮
D
G
D/F♯
mid A♯
It gets a lit - tle lone - ly, all these emp - ty rooms, just
F♯7
Bm/D
E
watch - ing the hours tick by.
mid A♮
A♯
C♯
A♮
G♯
Tap on soundboard or body of harp to sound like a ticking clock
D
Dsus
D
Dsus
D
Dsus
Gmaj9
middle C♯
G♮

Slower, tenderly
mp
Dsus2
Asus2/C♯
Please, I know you're in there. Peo - ple are ask ing where you've been.
G
Bm
They say, "Have cour - age," and I'm try - ing to; I'm right out here for you, just let me
F♯m
G
in. We on - ly have each oth - er; it's just
G♯
G♮
A/C♯
D
Bm
C♯dim7
Bm
E7
you and me. What are we gon - na do?
A♯
A♮
G♯
N.C.
D/F♯
G
N.C.
rit.
Do you want to build a snow - man?
Damp the lower strings
G♮

Heimr Árnadalr

From Disney FROZEN

Music by CHRISTOPHE BECK
Lyrics by CHRISTINE HALS

Harp arrangement by SYLVIA WOODS

Lever harp players: Set your levers for the Fs as shown above.
The other F strings on your harp are not needed, so can be set either natural or sharp.

This piece requires 20 strings, from a G up to an E. It can be played on many lap harps, if you play everything an octave higher than written.

This beautiful piece was sung by a choir during Elsa's coronation scene in the movie. The Icelandic lyrics are the top line, with a phonetic version below.

Slowly

Ver - ðug drót - tning stór Hjar - taaf gu - li skín - na.
Wer - thoog drawt - ning stor Yar - taf goo - li skeen - na

Kró - num þik með vo - num ást og trú.
Crow - noom theek meth vo - num aost og true

F♮

Fag - ra grýtt - ur land hei - mr Ár - na - dalr Fyl - gið
Fah - gra grytt - or land hey - mr Are - na - dalr Phyl - gith